YOUNG SCIENTIST CONCEPTS & PROJECTS

RAIN FORESTS

JEN GREEN

Gareth Stevens Publishing
MILWAUKEE

The original publishers would like to thank the following children for modeling in this book: Dulguk Batkhishig, Winnie Collate, Kira Dunleavy Brackett, Roxanne Game, Joshua Jenkins, Daniel Haston, Kieron Minto, Hector Mendez, Gemma Nelson, and Paul Payne.

**For a free color catalog describing Gareth Stevens' list
of high-quality books and multimedia programs,
call 1-800-542-2595 (USA) or 1-800-461-9120 (Canada).
Gareth Stevens Publishing's Fax: (414) 225-0377.**

Library of Congress Cataloging-in-Publication Data

Green, Jen.
Rain forests / by Jen Green.
p. cm. — (Young scientist concepts and projects)
Includes bibliographical references and index.
Summary: Describes the world's rain forests, their canopies and forest floors,
their climate, and the variety of plants and animals which they support.
Includes related projects and activities.
ISBN 0-8368-2268-4 (lib. bdg.)
1. Rain forest ecology—Study and teaching—Activity programs—
Juvenile literature. 2. Rain forests—Study and teaching—Activity programs—
Juvenile literature. [1. Rain forests. 2. Rain forest ecology. 3. Ecology.
4. Rain forests—Experiments. 5. Experiments.] I. Title. II. Series.
QH541.5.R27G74   1999
577.34'078—dc21   98-45665

This North American edition first published in 1999 by
Gareth Stevens Publishing
1555 North RiverCenter Drive, Suite 201
Milwaukee, WI 53212 USA

Original edition © 1998 by Anness Publishing Limited.
First published in 1998 by Lorenz Books, an imprint of
Anness Publishing Inc., New York, New York.
This U.S. edition © 1999 by Gareth Stevens, Inc.
Additional end matter © 1999 by Gareth Stevens, Inc.

Project editor: Sophie Warne
Editor: Charlotte Hurdman
Consultants: David Burnie and James Fairhead
Special photography: John Freeman
Stylist: Melanie Williams
Designer: Ann Samuel
Illustrators: Stephen Sweet/Simon Girling Associates
and Alan Male/Linden Artists
Gareth Stevens series editor: Dorothy L. Gibbs
Editorial assistant: Diane Laska

Printed in the United States of America

1 2 3 4 5 6 7 8 9 03 02 01 00 99

RAIN FORESTS

CONTENTS

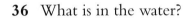
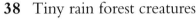

WHAT IS A RAIN FOREST?

RAIN forests are the most lush and fertile places on Earth. They are home to an amazing variety of plant and animal life. The best-known rain forests are tropical forests. They are found in a belt around the equator, in an area called the tropics. The sun's rays strike Earth so fiercely and directly in the tropics that the climate is always hot there. Rain forests are also found outside the tropics in temperate parts of the world, where the climate is cooler. Both tropical and temperate rain forests receive at least 78 inches (1,981 millimeters) of rainfall each year and have many trees that are more than 100 feet (30 meters) tall. The varieties of plant and animal life found in each type of rain forest, however, are very different.

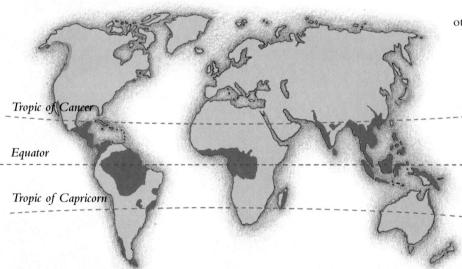

Tropic of Cancer

Equator

Tropic of Capricorn

Light and shade
In a rain forest, the trees and other plants spread their leaves to capture as much sunlight as possible. Together the leaves form a kind of roof, called the canopy. Animals are hard to see in this thick cover.

Rain forest places
This map *(left)* shows, in dark green, the locations of the world's tropical rain forests. Tropical and temperate rain forests cover only a small part of Earth's surface — about six percent, yet they are home to over half the species of plants and animals in the world.

Forest stories

Rain forests are made up of four different stories, or layers. The canopy is the dense, leafy layer at the top. The tallest trees, which rise above the forest canopy, are called emergents. The understory is the layer between the canopy and the ground. The lowest layer is the forest floor.

Emergent trees rise above the canopy.

The forest canopy forms a dense roof.

Understory plants thrive in shady places.

Fewer plants grow on the forest floor.

RAIN FORESTS OF THE WORLD

THERE are several types of rain forests. Tropical rain forests are found near the equator. It is warm and wet there all year round. Daytime temperatures remain steady at about 86° Fahrenheit (30° Celsius), and rain falls almost every afternoon. Trees and other plants thrive in these constant temperatures. Cooler temperate rain forests are found outside the tropics. Here, temperatures are more varied and conditions are less constant. Most tropical forests are found in lowland areas. Lowland forest becomes montane, or cloud, forest on upland slopes and mangrove forest at the coast and along rivers. Flooded forest is found alongside rivers that overflow their banks for several weeks each year. The divisions between different types of rain forests can be distinct, but sometimes the types merge into each other with no clear division.

Flowers of the forest
Bright flowers bloom among the dense foliage of a tropical rain forest. Trees and other plants thrive in the warm, moist conditions found all year round in tropical lowland forests.

Cloud forests
Montane forests are found on hills and mountains, where conditions are cooler and damper than in lowland forests. The upper slopes of montane forests are always hidden in mist and fog, so they are also known as cloud forests.

Lowland rain forests
Most tropical rain forests are found in lowland areas. Plants and animals are most abundant in the canopy and the understory layers.

Flooded forests
Strips of land along the banks of slow-flowing rivers are covered with flooded forests. The rivers regularly burst their banks and flood the forest floor. Although some flooded forests are permanently underwater, many kinds of trees and other plants still flourish there. The fertile soil is enriched with silt carried downstream by the river when it floods.

Temperate forests
Moss and ferns flourish on maple trees in the temperate rain forest along the northwestern coast of North America. Daily temperatures vary more in temperate rain forests than in tropical rain forests, but there is still plenty of rain. Temperate forests contain some of the world's tallest and oldest trees.

Mangrove forests
Swampy forests, called mangrove forests, are found along tropical coastlines and river estuaries, where the soil is rich in silt and mud. Mangroves have their roots in salty water, which is low in oxygen, so they put out special roots above the surface to breathe.

THE TOPMOST TREES

Skillful climbers
Small monkeys, such as this capuchin *(above)*, are very agile. They scramble and leap among tree branches, using their tails to help them balance. Some monkeys can even wind their tails around the branches.

Emergent layer
Tall emergent trees rise above the Amazon rain forest canopy in Brazil. Emergents have long, straight trunks and leafy crowns that spread out like umbrellas. One of the tallest emergents, the tualang tree, can grow up to 230 feet (70 m) above the ground. It is found in Southeast Asia.

R AIN forest trees grow very tall, up to heights of 165 feet (50 m). High above the ground, their leaves spread out to form the forest canopy. Stretching above the canopy are emergents, which grow up to 230 feet (70 m) high. Emergents are the tallest trees in the rain forest. The canopy is home to many smaller plants, such as orchids and bromeliads. These plants grow and flower high above the ground, but they are not rooted in forest soil. Instead, they root onto the branches of forest trees. Plants that grow on other plants without harming them are known as epiphytes, or air plants. Many air plants have leaves with a smooth, waxy surface to prevent them from losing too much water. Colorful birds and nimble monkeys live among these plants. They are small, lightweight animals; the slender twigs and stems of the plants would not support heavier ones.

Conure

This noisy, brightly colored bird *(below)* is a species of parrot, called a conure. Conures live in the rain forest canopy, fluttering from tree to tree, gorging themselves on fruits, seeds, flowers, and insects. They use their hooked beaks to tear apart fruit, crack open seeds, and even to help them climb.

Walking in the air

Because it is very difficult to reach the species of the upper canopy to study them, scientists knew little about the plants and animals there, until recently. Now, scientists string walkways between high tree trunks or build tall observation towers.

Air plant

This pink orchid *(below)* is growing on a rain forest tree in Brazil. It is an epiphytic air plant, which means it grows on the tree but is not a parasite. The orchid does not take food or water from the host tree. It simply uses that tree as a stepping-stone to reach the light.

Drip tips

In the upper canopy, the leaves of many plants have a special shape that tapers to a point called a drip tip. This shape allows excess water to run off the plant after a heavy rain, helping to prevent harmful algae from growing on the leaves.

FOREST SURVEY

Kauri pines
Kauris grow in the temperate rain forest of New Zealand. Like many trees, their trunks are distinctive, growing tall and straight to reach the light.

A small area of rain forest holds many different species, or kinds, of trees. In some rain forests, you can walk for more than an hour without coming across the same species twice. One of the first jobs for scientists working in a rain forest is to identify all the trees in their study area. Both in the rain forest and in your local area, trees can be identified by looking at their general size and shape. You can also study their bark, leaves, and flowers and look for other clues, such as fruits and nuts. In tropical rain forests, most trees stay green all year round. In countries with a temperate (moderate) climate, many trees shed their leaves in autumn. The shape of a tree's trunk and branches can also help identify it. When studying trees, scientists record their girth, or distance around the trunk, measuring at chest height. You can survey and identify the trees in a local park or woods using the same methods. Choose a wooded area with many different kinds of trees. Always take an adult with you for safety.

You will need: field guide, notebook, pen, colored pencils.

Identifying trees

1 As you walk along a path in the woods, use a field guide to help you identify, by general height and shape, the trees you see there.

2 Bark can help identify some trees. This birch bark is smooth and white with dark cracks. Match the bark with pictures in the field guide.

3 Study leaf shapes, fruits, and seeds. Record the trees you identify in a notebook. Add colored drawings, too.

A leaf from a sycamore tree

Seeds from a linden tree

An acorn and its cupule from an oak tree

A chestnut and its spiny covering from a horse chestnut tree

Seeds from a maple tree

Hips and leaves from a cockspur hawthorn tree

MATERIALS

You will need: tape, long piece of string, gloves, ruler or tape measure, pen, notebook, colored pencils, field guide, graph paper.

Make a chart, with drawings of the trees you find, on which to record their girths.

1 square = 2 inches (5 cm)
Evergreen
Beech
Horse chestnut
Cherry
Birch

Measure a tree's girth

1 Put a piece of tape on the string. Wrap the string around a tree trunk at chest height. Mark with your finger where the string and tape meet.

2 Lay the string along a ruler to measure the length from your finger to the piece of tape. This measurement is the girth of the tree.

3 Measure the girths of other trees and record them on a chart. The trees with thicker trunks are usually older than those with slender trunks.

RAIN FOREST CANOPY

Plants of the understory
Understory plants include shrubs and smaller trees, such as palms. Epiphytes and climbers festoon the branches.

THE trees of the rain forest canopy form a dense, leafy layer 165 feet (50 m) above the ground and up to 50 feet (15 m) thick. The canopy catches most of the rain and sunlight. The understory below the canopy is drier and shadier. Epiphytes, such as ferns and bromeliads, grow in both layers. Vines and climbing lianas twist up from the forest floor toward the light. Both the canopy and the understory are home to a variety of animals. Bats, birds, and flying insects flit among the branches, gathering food. Most animals that cannot fly are good climbers. Some, such as flying squirrels and flying lizards, can glide between the trees. Others visit the canopy only when they climb to the treetops from the ground. Some creatures spend their entire lives in the branches, rarely dropping down to the forest floor.

Tamandua
This mammal's favorite food is termites. The tamandua *(above)* uses its long snout and sticky tongue to probe inside termite nests to lick out the insects. Sharp claws and a long tail help it clamber among the branches of the canopy.

Macaws
Macaws *(right)* are brightly colored parrots. They use their powerful, hooked beaks to crack open nuts and seeds. Their short wings help them fly and maneuver through the crowded canopy.

Bromeliads

The branches of this rain forest tree in Brazil *(right)* are covered with bromeliads. High in the air, without roots in the soil, bromeliads must conserve, or save, as much moisture as possible. Some bromeliads collect rainwater in cups formed from rings of their waxy leaves. Insects and tiny frogs live, and even breed, in these small pools.

Climbing lianas

Lianas *(right)* are climbing plants with long, slender stems. They use the trunks of trees for support as they spiral upward toward the light. At the top, they put out leaves, shoots, and colorful flowers. Some lianas send down special roots, called aerial roots, to gather nourishing minerals from the soil. These roots may thicken and become gnarled, woody stems.

Strangler figs

This climbing plant *(left)* eventually kills the host tree that supports it. A young fig lives high in the branches. As it grows, it sends down roots to the forest floor. The roots spread and then put out branches that twine around the host tree, enclosing it. Eventually the host dies, rotting away to leave a hollow network of fig stems.

PLANTS OF THE CANOPY

Plants cannot move around to find food the way animals do. Instead, they make their own food. The leaves and stems of plants are green because they contain a substance called chlorophyll. Their green cells work like tiny solar panels, using the energy from sunlight to combine carbon dioxide gas from the air and water from the ground to produce the plant's sugary food and oxygen. This amazing process is called photosynthesis. In a rain forest, plants of the canopy and understory are in competition for light. When a tree or branch falls, plants and seedlings grow quickly, each rushing to spread its leaves in the extra light. A similar search for light can be seen in the experiment on this page with watercress seedlings. To get closer to the light, epiphytes, such as bromeliads, perch on high branches. Find out more about epiphytes, or air plants, by growing them at home.

Leaves take in
carbon dioxide.

Sunlight provides the energy for photosynthesis.

Chlorophyll in the leaves combines carbon dioxide and water.

Roots take in water and minerals.

Through photosynthesis, plants use the energy in sunlight to make their own food.

M A T E R I A L S

Reaching for the light

You will need: paper towels, water, 2 small plastic seed trays, watercress seeds, watering can.

1 Put a damp paper towel on the bottom of each seed tray. Sprinkle watercress seeds sparingly on top of the towels.

2 Store both trays in the dark for a few days until the watercress sprouts. Water the seeds regularly. Then, move one tray to a sunny place and leave the other tray in the dark.

Grown in a sunny place, seedlings are thick and healthy.

Left in the dark, seedlings grow tall and spindly to reach any light.

Grow your own air plant

1 Wearing gloves, wrap moss around one end of a branch or a piece of driftwood. Tie the moss securely in place with thread.

2 Put gravel into a sturdy flowerpot until the pot is almost full. You could use a trowel to transfer the gravel.

3 Push the branch or driftwood into the gravel so it will stand up in the pot without tipping the pot over. Spray the moss with water.

M A T E R I A L S

You will need: gloves, sphagnum moss, branch or piece of driftwood, thread, gravel, flowerpot, trowel, water sprayer, air plants (from a garden center), glue, liquid plant food.

5 Spray the plants with water occasionally. Add a few drops of liquid plant food in the water to help them grow.

Air plants grow well indoors and make an unusual display. They do not need soil to grow; instead, they wrap their roots around a branch.

4 Arrange air plants on the branch by pressing them gently into the moss. A drop of glue on the base of each plant will help hold it in place.

THE FOREST FLOOR

THE floor of the rain forest is dim and shady. The dense, leafy canopy blocks out most of the light. The plants of the canopy also absorb much of the water. After a heavy rain shower, it can take as long as ten minutes for water to drip down through the leaves to the ground. Where sunlight reaches the ground along the banks of rivers and in forest clearings, the undergrowth is dense and lush. Elsewhere, the lack of light keeps many plants and shrubs from living at ground level. You might think the soil in a tropical rain forest would be rich and fertile. In fact, it becomes thin and poor, because the rain forest plants quickly use up all the nutrients in the soil. The ground is covered with a thick carpet of fallen leaves. The leaves rot quickly, broken down by insects and other tiny creatures. The rotting process enriches the soil. In dappled light, larger animals, such as tapir, small deer, and rodents, sift through the leaves in search of food.

Plants of the forest floor
Ferns and flowering plants (*above*) thrive in pools of sunlight created by a fallen tree. Elsewhere, it is too shady for most plants to flourish. Fungi and parasitic plants (those that feed off other plants), however, thrive in dim light.

The scarlet flowers of this heliconia (left) make a bright splash of color in a forest clearing in Cuba. When a mighty forest tree falls, other plants are quick to take advantage of the increased light.

Buttress roots
In most rain forests, only a thin layer of soil covers the ground. To anchor themselves firmly, large trees grow special roots, called buttress roots (*left*). Thin wings of very hard wood rise from roots in the ground and act as buttresses to support the tree's weight.

Python

The orange and black markings on this python *(above)* help hide it among fallen leaves on the forest floor. Camouflage is an important weapon as the python lies in wait for prey. Pythons are constrictors, which means they kill their prey by wrapping themselves around their victims and squeezing them to death.

Tapir

The tapir *(above)* uses its long, flexible, upper lip to tear leaves and shoots from plants as it browses in the undergrowth. These shy, piglike animals are active mainly at night.

Parasitic plant

The *Balanophora elongata (below)* is a parasitic plant that grows on the roots of rain forest trees in Southeast Asia. It attaches itself to the host plant's roots, then steals that plant's food and water. Because it does not make its own food, it does not need green leaves or sunlight.

STUDYING THE FOREST FLOOR

Studying plant life

Botanists (scientists who study plants) take samples and measure the depth of the leaf layer in the Amazon rain forest. Creatures feeding on the forest floor help release the nutrients contained in dead leaves and fallen branches.

TROPICAL rain forests are amazingly rich in plant and animal life. As many as fifty plant species can grow on just one tree, and new species of plants are being identified every week. Biologists working in rain forests use a square frame called a quadrat to help them record all the plants living in a patch of forest soil. With an adult, you can use the same method to survey plant life in woods or a forest nearby. Beneath the ground, a forest teems with life. Creatures, such as worms, slugs, millipedes, and beetles, burrow through the soil. Much smaller creatures, such as mites, also live here. All these creatures feed on dead plant and animal matter. Bacteria and fungi break down everything that remains, helping to create a rich fertilizer for the plants. As leaves rot, they return nutrients to the soil. Leaves and other plant material decay quickest in warm, moist areas.

MATERIALS

You will need: gloves, 8 tent stakes, ruler or tape measure, string, field guide, pen, notebook, colored pencils, graph paper.

Do a plant survey

1 Find a patch of ground to sample and push in a stake. Measure 3 feet (1 m) and push in another stake. Connect the stakes with string.

2 Measure each remaining side to make one square yard (square meter). Push in two more stakes and connect the stakes with string.

3 Measure each side and mark the midpoint with stakes. Connect these stakes with string to divide the square into quarters.

4 Use a field guide to help you identify the plant species growing in each quarter of the square. Keep this information in a notebook.

Plant survey chart

5 Draw a chart on graph paper to show the position of each plant in each quarter. Use a different color for each type of plant on the chart.

MATERIALS

You will need: gloves, trowel, 2 plastic containers (one with a lid), soil, dead leaves, watering can.

After a few weeks, the leaves in the wet soil (left) will have started to rot, while those in the dry soil (right) will have shriveled.

Watching decay in the soil

1 Be sure to wear gloves for this project. Use a trowel to fill two plastic containers with plenty of dry soil.

2 Put dead leaves on top of the soil in one container. Water the leaves and the soil thoroughly, then cover the container with a lid.

3 Put dead leaves on top of the soil in the other container, but do not add water or cover the container. Store both containers in a dry place.

LIFE-GIVING FORESTS

Rain forests cover only a tiny fraction of Earth's surface, yet they affect the air we breathe and influence weather patterns around the world. During photosynthesis, trees and plants take in carbon dioxide from the air and give off oxygen. Humans, and all other animals, need oxygen to breathe. Rain forests help maintain the right balance of gases in our atmosphere. They also act like giant sponges. When it rains, they soak up water that would otherwise run straight into rivers and out to sea. The trees take in moisture through their roots and release it again later, into the air, in the form of a gas called water vapor. High in the air, tiny drops of water gather to form clouds, which bring rain. By helping cause rain, forests bring life to drier areas. If rain forests are cut down, clouds will not gather and less rain will fall. Drought and crop failure might follow, even in areas hundreds of miles (kilometers) away.

Torrential rain
Heavy rain is common in tropical rain forests. The roots of trees and plants absorb much of the water. The rest trickles away to feed streams and rivers.

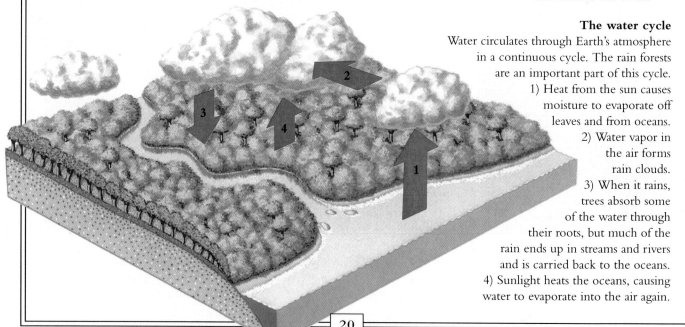

The water cycle
Water circulates through Earth's atmosphere in a continuous cycle. The rain forests are an important part of this cycle.
1) Heat from the sun causes moisture to evaporate off leaves and from oceans.
2) Water vapor in the air forms rain clouds.
3) When it rains, trees absorb some of the water through their roots, but much of the rain ends up in streams and rivers and is carried back to the oceans.
4) Sunlight heats the oceans, causing water to evaporate into the air again.

Mirror effect

The rain forest canopy is like a dark green blanket. Dark colors absorb more sunlight and heat than light colors do. Where parts of the forest are cut down, light-colored vegetation grows. This vegetation reflects more light, warming up the atmosphere.

Oxygen given off

Carbon dioxide taken in

During photosynthesis, trees and plants take in carbon dioxide and give off oxygen.

Keeping the air fresh
Trees help keep levels of oxygen consistent in Earth's atmosphere — the reverse of what humans and animals do as their lungs breathe in oxygen and breathe out carbon dioxide.

The greenhouse effect

Burning vegetation releases carbon dioxide and other gases into the air. These gases trap the sun's heat in the atmosphere, like glass does in a greenhouse, causing world temperatures to rise. This effect is called global warming.

Melting ice

Glaciers, like this one *(above)* in Antarctica, might well be affected by the burning of rain forests thousands of miles (km) away. If global warming continues, glaciers and ice caps in the Arctic and Antarctic will start to melt. As a result, sea levels around the world will rise, threatening low-lying coastal areas with flooding.

RAIN FOREST PLANTS

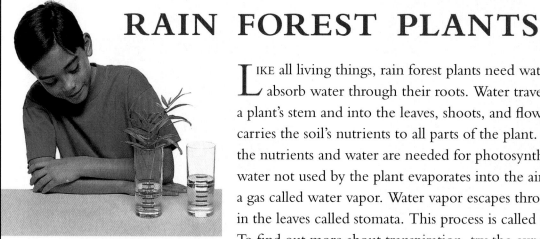

LIKE all living things, rain forest plants need water to live. They absorb water through their roots. Water travels up through a plant's stem and into the leaves, shoots, and flowers. Water carries the soil's nutrients to all parts of the plant. In the leaves, the nutrients and water are needed for photosynthesis. The excess water not used by the plant evaporates into the air in the form of a gas called water vapor. Water vapor escapes through tiny holes in the leaves called stomata. This process is called transpiration. To find out more about transpiration, try the experiment below. Using colored water, it shows how the water travels straight up a plant's stem, not across it. The water travels in tough-walled tubes, called xylem. The flower used here is a carnation, but this experiment will work just as well with a pale-colored daisy or a chrysanthemum.

Taking in water

Half-fill two glasses with water and mark the water level. Add some oil. (The oil will float on top.) Put a twig in one glass. If you check the water levels the next day, the water in the twig's glass will be lower. Water cannot evaporate through oil, so we know that the twig has taken it in.

M A T E R I A L S

You will need: 2 tall glasses, water, water-soluble ink or food coloring, white carnation, tape, scissors.

Transpiration in color

1 Half-fill two tall glasses with water. Add a few drops of ink or food coloring to one glass to give the water a bright color.

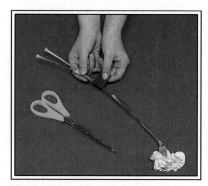

2 Split the stem of the carnation to about halfway up. Wrap the stem with tape at that point, so it does not split any further.

3 Place the glasses side by side and stand one half of the carnation's stem in each glass.

4 After a few hours, check the carnation to see what has happened. Half of the flower will be colored; the other half will still be white.

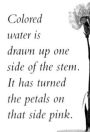

Colored water is drawn up one side of the stem. It has turned the petals on that side pink.

M A T E R I A L S

You will need: houseplant, watering can, clear plastic bag, tape, scissors.

Moisture, given off by the plant as water vapor, condenses, or turns back to water, when it touches the sides of the plastic bag.

Evaporation in action

1 Water the houseplant well, using a watering can. Watering the plant from the base is best, or water just the soil.

2 Carefully put a plastic bag over the plant and tape it tightly around the pot. Leave the bag on the plant overnight.

3 Inside the bag, water vapor given off by the plant turns back into water. The air inside is warm and moist, like the air in a rain forest.

RAIN FOREST CYCLES

LIKE most plants and trees, those that grow in the rain forest reproduce from seeds. To make seeds, plants must be fertilized with pollen, usually from another plant of the same species. Most rain forest plants are pollinated by animals — mainly insects, such as bees and butterflies, but also birds and even bats. Animals are attracted to the sugary nectar the plants produce and to the bright colors and strong scents of their flowers. When an animal reaches into a flower to feed on nectar, pollen rubs off on its body. The pollen is transferred to the next plant the creature visits and fertilizes that plant. After fertilization, a plant makes seeds, which must be spread around as much as possible. The seeds of some plants are spread by water, and a few are carried on the wind. Most plants, however, rely on animals to spread their seeds. Seeds often develop inside juicy fruits. When an animal eats the fruit, it spits out the seeds or passes them in its droppings, sometimes far away from the parent plant.

Insect partners
Some plants are pollinated by many different kinds of insects. Orchids, however, are often pollinated by a single species — usually bees. To attract bees, orchids are brightly colored and have special scents; some are even shaped like bees.

Bird helpers
When a tiny hummingbird reaches inside a flower with its long beak and tongue, its beak and body are dusted with pollen grains. Plants pollinated by birds often produce brightly colored flowers, because birds see bright colors clearly.

FACT BOX

• To hover in front of flowers to feed, hummingbirds beat their wings up to eighty times a second — faster than the human eye can see. The humming sound of their fluttering wings gives these birds their name.

• The sausage tree of Madagascar is pollinated by bats. The tree is named for the shape of its fruits.

• Sago palm trees produce fruits inside scaly cases with a corky layer so that the fruit can float on water. These trees die after they have produced fruit.

Blowing in the wind

The kapok is one of the few rain forest trees from which the seeds *(above)* are spread by wind. These tall trees rise above the canopy, where there are more air currents. When a kapok pod splits open, the tuft of threads inside carries the tiny seeds away on the wind.

Night pollinators

Some plants are pollinated by fruit bats *(above)* or moths, which are active at dusk or when it is dark. The flowers of these plants open at night and have strong scents to attract these animals. Brightly colored flowers are less effective at night, because their colors do not show up in the dark.

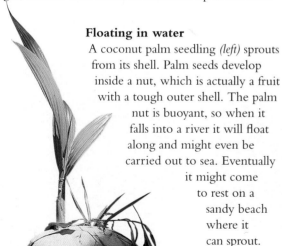

Floating in water

A coconut palm seedling *(left)* sprouts from its shell. Palm seeds develop inside a nut, which is actually a fruit with a tough outer shell. The palm nut is buoyant, so when it falls into a river it will float along and might even be carried out to sea. Eventually it might come to rest on a sandy beach where it can sprout. Some palm nuts travel thousands of miles (km).

Traveling seeds

Pacas *(left)* are rodents from Central and South America. They forage at night for roots, seeds, fruits, and berries on the forest floor. Seeds pass through the animal unharmed and come out later in its droppings. With their ready-made packet of fertilizer, these seeds root and grow quickly.

LOOKING AT PLANT CYCLES

M A T E R I A L S

You will need: gloves, field guide, collecting jar, notebook, colored pencils.

The plants where you live disperse, or spread, their seeds the same ways rain forest plants do. If you take a close look at seeds, you will be able to tell how they are spread. All over the world, you can find plants that produce seeds inside plump, juicy fruits. When birds and mammals eat the fruits, they spread the seeds. Other plants produce fruits with tiny hooks that can catch in an animal's fur. These fruits can be carried some distance before they drop off onto the ground and take root. Some plants produce light seeds that drift in the air, especially plants in temperate areas, which are often windier than rain forests. Once seeds are spread, they germinate (take root and grow) if the light, warmth, and moisture conditions are right. On the shady rain forest floor, seeds might wait years before a tree crashes down and leaves a space with enough light for the seeds to grow. Indoors, in warm conditions, it is fairly easy to get rain forest seeds to grow. Try germinating an avocado plant from its pit, but make sure the atmosphere is warm and humid enough.

Looking at seed dispersal

1 In woods and parks, look for nuts and acorns that have been nibbled on. These seeds are nutritious food for many animals. Squirrels bury stores of seeds, which might germinate later.

2 Visit a pond or a stream to find seeds, such as alders, that are dispersed by water. Use a field guide to identify any seeds you see floating on the water.

3 Maple trees have light seeds with wings. The wings spin the seeds through the air, helping them fly far from the parent tree before they germinate.

4 Some plants, such as dandelions, have light seeds that are carried away by the wind. Each seed has its own small parachute of fine threads.

5 The capsules of poppies are like pepper shakers with hundreds of tiny seeds inside. As the wind shakes the capsules, the seeds spill out.

6 When you walk through tall grass or brush, you might find fruits with tiny hooks, called burrs, stuck to your coat or to a pet's fur. Burrs can be carried a long way before they rub off.

MATERIALS

You will need: avocado pit, 3 toothpicks, glass jar, water, gloves, flowerpot, trowel, soil mix.

Growing plants from tropical seeds

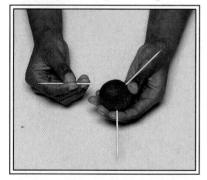

1 An avocado pit is the seed of an avocado plant. Clean off any fruit left on the pit, then carefully push three toothpicks into the pit *(as shown above)*.

2 Fill a glass jar with water and suspend the pit over the jar so it just touches the waterline. Keep the jar in a warm, dark place and add water regularly.

3 When roots begin to grow, plant the pit in a flowerpot filled with soil mix. Place the pot where the air is warm and humid and wait for the seedling to grow.

THE THREATENED FOREST

ALL around the world, rain forests are being cut down at an alarming rate. At the beginning of the twentieth century, these forests covered twice the area they do today. Recently, the pace of destruction has increased. Experts estimate that an area of rain forest about the size of England is lost each year. There are many reasons for this loss. One of the main reasons is logging — cutting down trees for timber. Many rain forest trees are valuable hardwoods, such as teak and mahogany, used for building houses and making furniture. Hardwood trees grow slowly and cannot be replaced quickly. Trees are also cut down to clear new pastureland for cattle. Poor-quality rain forest soil is quickly exhausted by farming, so more land must be cleared. When roads are cut through forests, large areas are disturbed.

Carted away
Giant logs are loaded onto a truck in Papua New Guinea to be carried to the nearest port or paper mill. Rich businessmen make large profits from the timber trade; local people receive very little.

Cut down for fuel
Many developing countries depend on rain forests for fuel and firewood. Here *(above)*, a kiln is being built to turn trees into charcoal, which is a better, more efficient fuel.

Cabbage crop
This field in Malaysia *(above)* was cleared from forest land for growing cabbages. Forest soil is too poor to grow crops for long. Within a few years, the soil will be exhausted.

Terraced rice fields

Hilly forest land in Indonesia *(left)* has been cleared and built up into terraces to grow rice. All over Southeast Asia, rain forest has been cut down to make rice paddies. Terraces have been built for centuries, but, now, this region's growing population puts greater pressure on forestland.

Cattle ranching

Land that is not fertile enough for crops is often sold to cattle ranchers for use as grazing land. In a few years, however, even the grass is of such poor quality that the cattle must be moved to fresh pastures. Land that once sustained a rain forest and all its animals and plants becomes useless.

Mining

A gold mine in Brazil *(above)* scars forestland. Mining is another major cause of forest destruction. International corporations dig for oil, coal, and valuable ores (metal-bearing rocks) as well as precious metals, such as gold and silver. As with the logging industry, large companies make big profits at the expense of the land and local people.

THE SELF-SUFFICIENT FOREST

You will need: potted plant, flowerpot filled with compost or soil, 2 plastic cups, 2 watering cans.

WHEN rain forest trees are cut down, even the soil is threatened. The roots of trees and plants help hold the thin forest soil together. When the soil is left bare, it can be washed away by heavy rainfall. This loss of soil is called erosion. The project on this page will show you how erosion occurs. When rain forests are left alone, they sustain themselves indefinitely, recycling water and nutrients from the soil. To see how this recycling works, grow a mini-rain forest in a large bottle. The bottle reproduces the warm, moist conditions found in the rain forest. Inside the bottle, plants are kept at an even temperature and are protected from drafts. They recycle their own moisture, so they rarely need watering.

Destructive deforestation
Soil washes quickly off hillsides, like these *(above)* in Madagascar, that were once covered with rain forest trees. The soil builds up downstream, clogging rivers and streams, which causes flooding along their banks.

Looking at soil erosion

1 Fit the potted plant into the neck of one of the plastic cups. Place the pot of soil in the neck of the other cup.

2 Pour water into both pots. What happens?

Water passes quickly through the pot without the plant. The water is muddy because it is washing a lot of soil through with it.

Water passes more slowly through the pot with the plant. It trickles through almost clear.

Plant a mini-rain forest

1 Wash out the bottle or jar to make sure it is clean. Wearing gloves, put handfuls of gravel into the bottom of the bottle.

2 Combine a little charcoal and soil mix. Add a deep layer of this mixture to the bottle, smoothing out the top of the soil.

3 Make holes for the plants in the soil with a spoon or a trowel. Then, gently lower the plants into the holes.

M A T E R I A L S

You will need: large plastic bottle or jar with a lid, gloves, gravel, charcoal, soil mix, spoon or trowel, small tropical plants, plant sprayer (or watering can with sprinkler attachment).

Moisture from the plants will condense on the sides of the bottle and will drip down into the soil to be reused.

4 Pat the soil down around the base of each plant. Use a spoon or trowel if you cannot reach that far with your fingers.

5 Use a plant sprayer to mist the plants and soil thoroughly with water, or use a watering can with a sprinkler attachment.

6 Put the lid on the bottle. Your mini-rain forest is complete! Water is recycled inside the bottle, so you will not have to add water very often.

THE WEB OF LIFE

RAIN forests support a wide variety of life-forms in a web that contains thousands of plant and animal species. In a tropical rain forest, plant food is available all year round. Herbivores, or plant-eating animals, thrive on many kinds of vegetation, including leaves, shoots, flowers, fruits, and nuts. Carnivores, or meat-eating animals, prey on, or hunt, herbivores and weaker carnivores. Prey are constantly alert to the danger of being killed and eaten. To survive, carnivores must first find, then catch and kill, their prey. Animals that kill and eat other animals are called predators. They have keen senses to help them hunt. Predators use different means to catch their prey. Big cats, for example, rely on strength and speed to outrun their victims. Other hunters, such as snakes, use stealth to pounce on unsuspecting animals.

Bloodsucker
A vampire bat *(above)* preys on large mammals, such as cattle, but does not kill its victims. It uses its sharp front teeth to puncture the animal's skin, then sucks out the animal's blood. The bat's saliva prevents the blood from clotting during feeding.

Winged carnivore
A harpy eagle is a fierce predator that lives in the treetops. It preys on monkeys and small mammals it sees scrambling around in the branches, searching for fruit. The eagle swoops down and kills its prey with its sharp claws, or talons.

Food web
The links between life-forms in a tropical rain forest can be shown in a food web. At the bottom of the web are plants, which make their own food. Herbivores eat the plants and, in turn, may be eaten by carnivores. Animals that eat both plants and animals are called omnivores. This diagram *(left)* shows part of a food web in South America.

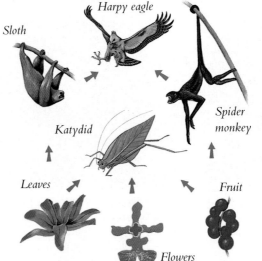

Harpy eagle

Sloth

Spider monkey

Katydid

Leaves

Fruit

Flowers

Plant-eater

In South American rain forests, sloths *(right)* hang from branches, feeding on leaves. Plant food is easy to find, but it is not very nourishing, so sloths have to save as much energy as possible. They save energy by moving very slowly and spending most of their time resting.

Since vipers cannot chew with their teeth, they swallow their prey whole.

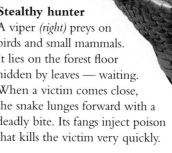

Top predator

A jaguar *(above)* preys on many different kinds of animals, including cattle, pigs, terrapins, and dogs. Its spotted coat helps it stay hidden as it tracks its prey. The jaguar is at the top of its food chain and has little to fear from other animals, except humans.

Stealthy hunter

A viper *(right)* preys on birds and small mammals. It lies on the forest floor hidden by leaves — waiting. When a victim comes close, the snake lunges forward with a deadly bite. Its fangs inject poison that kills the victim very quickly.

ANIMAL TRACKS

THE animals of a forest near you search for their food in ways similar to the animals of the rain forests. Wild creatures are very wary and will disappear into the forest at the slightest hint of danger. You can, however, learn a lot about animals by looking at their tracks. Ask an adult to take

you looking for footprints where there is soft mud or sand, or wherever the ground is wet. The banks of streams or rivers are often crisscrossed with animal prints. In winter, tracks are easy to see after a snowfall. Tracks can give clues about the size and weight of the animal that made them. They also show how animals move — whether they run, hop, slide, or slither.

These footprints (above) were made by an Asian elephant in the bottom of a dried-up riverbed.

You will need: gloves, field guide, magnifying glass, notebook, pencil, camera.

Compare the tracks you find to pictures in a field guide. Different groups of animals (mammals, birds, reptiles, and amphibians) leave very different tracks. Draw the footprints or take photographs and keep records of the tracks you find in a notebook. Try making a plaster cast of an animal print.

Looking at animal tracks

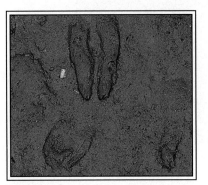

1 When you find a footprint, count the number of toes. Can you see any claws? A fox's paw is rounded, with four toes and claws.

2 Deer have narrow, split hooves with two toes. They leave deep tracks because they walk with all their weight on their toes.

3 Most birds have long, spindly feet, with three or four toes. Some wading birds have webbed feet, which leave distinctive prints.

Make a footprint cast

1 Find a clear animal track in sand or dry mud. Remove any debris from around the print. Always wear gloves when working with soil.

2 Bend a strip of heavy paper into a ring large enough to fit around the print. Secure it with a paper clip. Place the paper ring over the print.

3 Mix plaster of paris and water in a bowl (following instructions on the package). Stir the mixture until it is thick and even.

MATERIALS

You will need: strip of heavy paper, paper clip, plaster of paris, water, mixing bowl, spoon, trowel, scrub brush, paintbrush, paints.

Finished cast of a dog's footprint

4 Carefully spoon enough plaster of paris over the print to cover it. Wait about 15 minutes or until the plaster is completely dry.

5 Use a trowel to pry the cast loose. Peel off the paper ring. Clean the cast by brushing off any loose soil or sand.

6 Allow the cast to dry 24 hours, then paint or varnish it.

WHAT IS IN THE WATER?

WATER is everywhere in a tropical rain forest. It drips down from the canopy, forming swampy puddles in the soil, and feeds gushing streams and rivers. The world's second-longest river, the Amazon in South America, flows over 3,900 miles (6,300 km) from the Andes Mountains to the Atlantic Ocean. This river is home to five thousand species of fish, including the arapaima, the world's largest freshwater fish, and the deadly piranha. Water mammals, such as huge otters and capybaras, thrive along with many reptiles, including crocodiles, anacondas, and a lizard that walks on water. Where the river widens near the sea, dolphins and seal-like manatees live in its murky water.

The Amazon basin
The *igapó* and *várzea* are large areas of Amazon rain forest that flood regularly. The plants here live underwater for up to six months every year.

Piranhas
These river fish *(above)* have razor-sharp teeth. Although they live on seeds and fruit, they also eat meat and can be dangerous to humans. A school of piranhas can tear the flesh off an animal in minutes.

Capybaras
The world's largest rodents, called capybaras *(above),* look a little like giant guinea pigs. Capybaras live in family groups. With partly webbed feet, they are excellent swimmers and spend a lot of time in the water.

Basilisk lizards

The rain forests of South America are home to a remarkable reptile — a lizard that can walk on water. The basilisk lizard *(above)* has flattened, webbed toes with an extra fringe of scales. Using its tail for balance, the basilisk can drop onto water and run across the surface on its back legs to escape from a predator.

Anacondas

An anaconda *(below)* can grow up to 9 feet (3 m) long and weigh over 500 pounds (227 kilograms). These giant reptiles are one of the world's largest snakes. They are strong swimmers and spend much of their lives in the water. When hunting, they swim close to shore, searching for prey as large as deer. They kill their victims by strangling or drowning them.

Caimans

The caiman *(left)* is a kind of alligator found on the banks of rain forest rivers. It has a broad mouth for eating a wide variety of prey. When hunting, the caiman slides through the water with just its eyes and nostrils showing above the surface. When it sees an animal drinking on the riverbank, it approaches quietly, then pounces and seizes the victim's snout. It drags the animal underwater and holds it down until it drowns. A caiman will grab any prey it can find, and it will swallow fish and frogs whole.

TINY RAIN FOREST CREATURES

INSECTS are the most numerous species on Earth, making up more than three-quarters of all known creatures. Many species have not yet been named. Insects outnumber human beings two hundred million to one and are found in incredible numbers in tropical rain forests. Butterflies and bees live high in the rain forest canopy. Ants march along the branches of the understory. Beetles and other tiny creatures, such as spiders and centipedes, burrow among the leaves on the forest floor. Like larger forest animals, tiny creatures eat all kinds of foods. Many feed on plants, but some are predators, hunting other tiny creatures and even birds, small mammals, and reptiles. Beetles and worms crunch up decaying plants and animals in the forest soil. Tiny creatures are a vital food source for many larger animals. For protection, many of them are colored and patterned to blend in with the forest background. This method of disguise is called camouflage.

Golden beetle
The golden beetle *(above)* can be found in the cloud forest of Costa Rica in Central America. It feeds on ferns. When frightened, it lifts its tough, golden wing cases and spreads the delicate wings hidden underneath before flying away.

Leaf-cutter ants
These ants *(left)* scale the branches of tall trees to collect leaves. They use their sharp jaws to bite off sections of leaf, then carry the pieces back to their underground nest, often traveling over 325 feet (100 m). The ants chew the leaves into a pulp that is used to grow a special fungus on which they feed.

FACT BOX

• More than two thousand species of butterflies are found in the rain forests of South America.

• Leeches are sucking worms that fasten themselves firmly onto the skin of much larger animals to drink their blood. Once the leech has pierced a victim's skin, it releases a substance that prevents the animal's blood from clotting.

Flower mantis

This large insect *(above)* is a praying mantis. The color, shape, and pattern of its body exactly imitate a tropical orchid. It waits for its prey hidden against the flower. When an unwary creature comes too close, the mantis grabs it with its front legs and eats it alive.

Morpho butterfly

A morpho butterfly *(above)* suns itself by resting with its wings open on a leaf in the rain forest. Its bright blue color is produced by light reflecting off tiny scales on the surface of its wings.

Bird–eating spider

Large spiders, such as this Chilean bird-eating spider *(above)*, prey on birds, frogs, and reptiles, as well as insects. This spider bites its prey, injecting poison through hollow fangs. Other spiders spin silk thread and wrap it around a victim to immobilize it.

Katydid

This grasshopperlike insect *(above)* is a katydid from Costa Rica. The round markings on its wings are called eyespots. When threatened, the katydid raises its eyespots, hoping to convince the enemy that it is large and dangerous.

STUDYING TINY CREATURES

NATURALISTS who study insects and other small creatures in tropical rain forests have found an amazing variety of species. There are, in fact, so many species that some do not have a common name, only a scientific one. To identify all species living in a particular area, scientists mark off a quadrat, or square, and search all the possible places small creatures hide — under leaves, stones, and logs and in tiny crevices in tree trunks. They look for signs of feeding, such as chewed leaves or tiny holes in wood. Sometimes they leave pitfall traps in the ground or hang traps in trees. You can find and study small creatures using the same methods. Always wear gloves when handling them because some small creatures sting or bite. Better still, use a small paintbrush to handle them and to transfer them from your trap. A field guide can help you identify them. When you are finished with your creatures, carefully release them where you found them. Do not keep them captive for more than a few hours.

Swallowtail butterflies are found in many parts of the world. This one (above) is from South America. Butterflies feed on rotten fruit and plant nectar. Put an overripe apple outside. What kinds of insects come to feed on it?

MATERIALS

You will need: gloves, paintbrush, magnifying glass, field guide, collecting jar, notebook, pencil.

Finding tiny creatures

1 Creatures such as worms and snails can be found under rocks and stones. Gently replace the stones when you have finished your search.

2 Cracks in rotting wood often shelter centipedes and wood lice, or sow bugs. Gently lift rotting bark to find these creatures.

Make a pitfall trap

1 Ask an adult where you can dig and use a trowel to make a hole in damp soil. Make the hole just big enough for the glass jar to fit in it.

2 Place the jar in the hole and pat the soil down around the sides of it. Put small, fresh leaves in the bottom of the jar for bait.

3 Arrange small stones around the trap and balance a large flat stone on top to keep the trap from filling with rain. Leave the trap out overnight.

WARNING
Do not leave tiny creatures in a trap for more than a few hours, or they will die.

M A T E R I A L S
You will need: gloves, trowel, glass jar, small fresh leaves, small stones, large flat stone or tile, muslin cloth, rubber band, magnifying glass, field guide.

4 In the morning, remove the jar. Place a piece of muslin cloth over the top and secure it with a rubber band. Use a magnifying glass to study the creatures you have caught. A field guide can help you identify them.

5 When you are finished studying the creatures, release them near the place where you found them.

A centipede has many pairs of legs, one pair on each body segment. A millipede has two pairs of legs on each body segment.

Adult insects, such as this queen wasp, have bodies with three main sections and six legs. Most insects also have wings.

CENTRAL AMERICA

ENTRAL America forms a land bridge between the continents of North and South America. To the northeast lies the Caribbean Sea and the islands of Cuba, Hispaniola, and Jamaica. This region was once entirely covered with rain forest, but large areas have been cleared for cattle ranching and sugarcane plantations. Like rain forests, the jungles and mangrove swamps of Central America contain many plants and animals found nowhere else. The Caribbean islands are particularly rich in unique wildlife, because, in the past, there were few predators to hunt them there. Native plants of the region include many kinds of bromeliads and orchids and cocoa trees, the pods of which are used to make chocolate.

Monkeys, big cats, snakes, and lizards scramble or slither among the trees of the Central American jungle, an area famous for its numerous tropical birds, including many kinds of parrots. Some of these birds are now endangered because so many of them have been caught and sold as pets.

Quetzal
The quetzal's spectacular feathers have a metallic sheen. The male quetzal *(above)* has one of the longest tail plumes of any bird. This bird was held sacred by the ancient Aztecs and Maya, who worshiped it as the god of the air. Anyone who harmed a quetzal was put to death.

Green tree boa
A green tree boa *(left)* lurks in the crook of a forest tree. Its green skin camouflages it, allowing it to sneak up on prey, such as deer and rodents. It coils its body around the animal and squeezes the victim to death before swallowing it whole.

Howler monkey
The howler monkey *(above)* is named for its loud, hooting call. Male monkeys call the loudest, to warn other monkeys away from the patch of the forest where their group is feeding. The monkey's large voice box amplifies its call.

Kinkajou

A member of the raccoon family, the kinkajou *(right)* has yellowish fur and a long, prehensile tail. It uses its tail as a climbing aid to clamber around the canopy, looking for fruit, insects, or eggs to eat. The kinkajou can use its tail to hold onto branches, but it cannot leap from tree to tree the way monkeys can.

Rain forest plants of Central America

Climbing plants and epiphytes, such as this bromeliad *(left)*, flourish in the lush forests of Central America. Climbing plants include the vanilla orchid. Its pods produce the vanilla used to flavor foods such as ice cream. Other plants include guava, cassava, locust trees, pineapple (a type of bromeliad), and arrowroot.

Ocelot

The ocelot *(left)* lives in the rain forests of Central America. The spots and stripes on every ocelot's coat are different, making each cat as individual as a fingerprint. Many of these creatures have been killed for their beautiful fur, so they are now quite rare.

THE AMAZON

THE Amazon jungle in South America is the world's largest tropical rain forest. It covers the basin of the Amazon River, the world's second-longest river. As the Amazon flows to the sea, thousands of smaller rivers and streams flow into it, swelling its waters. In most places, this river is only a few miles (km) across, but it widens closer to the Atlantic Ocean, until its banks are over 37 miles (59.5 km) apart. Here the river looks like a sea. The Amazon rain forest is home to the greatest variety of plants and animals on Earth. One-fifth of all the world's plant and bird species and about one-tenth of all mammal species are found there. Many more species are waiting to be discovered and identified by scientists. Forest birds include the colorful ibis and the toucan with its enormous beak. Mammals that live in the forest include the predatory jaguar, the scaly armadillo, and the slow-moving sloth.

Amerindians (Indians of the Americas)
These Amerindian children (*above*) are bathing while their mothers wash clothes in the river. Many different groups of Amerindians live in the rain forest. They are used to the changing levels of the river at different times of the year. As the water rises and falls, they net fish and farm crops.

Scarlet ibis
The scarlet ibis (*left*) lives in swampy areas of the rain forest. It wades through the mud on its long, stiltlike legs, probing with its beak for frogs and fishes. For years, this bird has been hunted for its brilliant plumage.

Ginger flowers
This long-stemmed plant (*right*) grows throughout lowland areas of the Amazon rain forest. One species of ginger flower produces edible, knobby roots, which are used fresh, dried, pickled, or preserved to flavor foods. The shoots, leaves, and flowers can also be eaten raw or cooked.

Hoatzin

The hoatzin *(left)* nests in the mangrove forests of the Amazon. It is a clumsy bird, about the size of a chicken, and a poor flier. It can manage only short flights along the river. Young hoatzins have two tiny claws on the front of each wing, which they use to help them climb trees.

Armored armadillo

The armadillo *(below)* is a shy creature. It rests by day and comes out at night to root for worms and insects in the forest soil. This animal's body is covered with a protective layer of bony plates. When threatened, the armadillo rolls itself up into a tight, scaly ball.

Poison-arrow frog

The blue poison-arrow frog *(left)* is one of several South American species with very poisonous skin. The poison stops hungry predators from eating the frog. Amerindian hunters use the poison to tip their blowpipe darts for hunting.

Toco toucan

The toucan is a well-known rain forest bird. The toco toucan *(below)* has one of the largest beaks of any bird. Its beak allows the toucan to reach forest berries dangling beyond the reach of most other creatures. Because the beak is partly hollow, it is not as heavy as it looks.

AFRICA

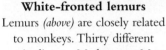

THE rain forests of Africa lie in a band across the west and center of the continent, on either side of the equator. In West Africa, the forest survives only in small pockets near the coast. It once contained many magnificent mahogany trees, but most of these tropical hardwoods have been cut down for their precious timber. Central Africa holds the world's second-largest rain forest. It contains areas of high cloud forest, mangrove swamps, and flooded forest, as well as lowland rain forest. A wide variety of plants and animals is found in these different habitats. The forest canopy is topped by tall, straight-trunked hardwood trees. Bamboo and palm trees grow in the understory. Many forest animals, including chameleons, okapi, and spotted leopards, rely on camouflage to hide from their enemies and sneak up on prey. To the southeast, the large island of Madagascar was once intensely forested. Now, however, much of this rain forest has been cut down. Madagascar is home to many plants and animals, such as the red-ruffed lemur and the rare serpent eagle, that are not found anywhere else.

White-fronted lemurs
Lemurs *(above)* are closely related to monkeys. Thirty different species live on Madagascar. Most roam the forest in small groups, looking for fruit and insects.

Chimpanzees
The lowland forests of Central Africa are an ideal habitat for chimpanzees *(left)*. These small apes are among the world's most intelligent creatures. They use stones as hammers and poke twigs inside termite nests to fish out the insects. Chimpanzees feed mainly on fruit and leaves, but they also eat meat. They make up organized hunting parties to catch pigs, deer, or smaller monkeys.

FACT BOX

• The rain forests of Central Africa are, by themselves, home to more than 8,000 different species of plants.

• Madagascar contains two-thirds of the world's chameleon species. These lizards have the amazing ability to change their skin color to match their surroundings by making different colored clumps of skin cells bigger or smaller.

Okapi
Okapi *(right)* live in lowland forests, feeding on leaves they tear off of plants with their long tongues. These large grazing animals are related to giraffes. Okapi have stripes on their legs and hide, which help them blend in with the forest's dappled vegetation, protecting them from predators.

Ground geckos
Geckos *(above)* are lizards. This one lives on the forest floor in Madagascar. Its body is camouflaged to disguise the lizard as it scuttles among the leaves.

Rain forest songbirds
Orioles are found in the rain forests of Africa and southern Asia, where they feed on fruit and insects. These birds are known for their beautiful song. This black-headed oriole *(left)* is keeping a sharp lookout for predators.

Hornbills
This red-billed hornbill *(left)* is preening its feathers to keep them clean and in good condition. Many kinds of hornbills live in lowland forests, where they make their nests in tree trunks. The male hornbill walls up the nest hole with mud to protect the female and the young inside from predators. He leaves a tiny hole through which he can feed his family.

SOUTHERN ASIA

THE rain forests of Asia stretch from India and Myanmar (Burma) in the west to Malaysia and the islands of Java and Borneo in the east. This area includes the Sundarbans in Bangladesh — one of the largest mangrove forests in the world. Most of mainland Asia has a subtropical climate with seasons of torrential monsoon rains. Southeast Asia is hot and humid all year round. Rain forest trees include rattan palms, rubber trees, and giant tropical hardwoods, such as teak, ebony, and rosewood. Other rain forest plants include bamboo, ginger, orchids, and rafflesia — the world's largest flower. Southeast Asian animals include gibbons, orangutans, and the rare Sumatran rhino. Indian rain forests are home to peacocks and deadly cobras. Elephants, tigers, and buffalo live in forest clearings. Large areas of Asian rain forest have been cut down for fuel or burned to make room for crops.

Peacock's display
A peacock *(above)* has the most spectacular tail feathers of any bird. When courting a female, or peahen, the male spreads its tail and quivers its fan of feathery eyes. Asian forests are also home to golden pheasants and red jungle fowl — the ancestor of the domestic chicken.

Giant rafflesia
Rafflesia *(below)*, the world's largest flower, blooms on the forest floor in Sumatra. This flower can measure up to 3 feet (1 m) across. It is a parasite that lives on the roots of some jungle vines. Rafflesia gives off a strong smell, like rotting meat, which attracts insects that pollinate the plant.

Hidden creatures
Rafflesia flowers are so huge that tiny mammals, such as this tree shrew *(above),* can take shelter inside. The flowers also provide a good source of the insects on which shrews feed.

Flying lizards

A flying lizard *(above)* has extra-long rib bones joined by a flap of skin. This flap can be spread like a frilly skirt, allowing the lizard to glide from tree to tree. Asian rain forests are home to a number of flying animals, including the colugo, or flying lemur, which has large flaps of skin along its body.

Gibbons

Gibbons swing from hand to hand, moving through treetops at great speed. This one *(above)* is hanging from a branch in Borneo.

Asian elephants

Unlike elephants of Africa, which inhabit open grasslands, elephants of Asia *(right)* live deep in the forest. They are smaller than their African relatives, with smaller ears, an arched back, and a domed forehead. Females and their young live in herds led by the oldest female, called the matriarch. They feed almost entirely on leaves.

FACT BOX

• The island of Java in Indonesia has lost ninety percent of its rain forest. Indonesia as a whole, however, still holds ten percent of the world's tropical rain forests.

• Flying animals of Asian rain forests include frogs, squirrels, and snakes. These creatures do not actually fly; instead, they glide through the air.

AUSTRALASIA

MILLIONS of years ago, Australia, New Zealand, and New Guinea formed a great forested southern continent isolated from the rest of the world. Today, these countries have many similar species of animals found nowhere else. In Australia, tropical rain forest survives only in a thin strip along the northeastern coast. Marsupials populate much of this area. Rain forest marsupials include tree kangaroos and sugar gliders. Female marsupials are known by the furry pouch in which they raise their young. North of Australia, the island of New Guinea is still mostly forested. Wildlife is a mix of species from Australia and Southeast Asia, including birds, such as cassowaries, bowerbirds, and birds of paradise. Mammals include the extraordinary, egg-laying echidna.

Australian rain forest
Undergrowth in Australia's tropical forests is dense and lush. The forests lie in the path of wet winds blowing in from the Pacific.

Cassowary
Like the ostrich, the cassowary *(right)* is a giant bird unable to fly. This ground-dweller lives in the forests of New Guinea. The large, bony crest on its head acts as a helmet as it crashes through the forest.

Sugar glider
The treetops of the Australian rain forest are home to a small, mouselike marsupial called a sugar glider *(above)*. It has two long, furry flaps of skin between its front and back legs. The animal stretches out its furry flaps to glide from tree to tree. It eats insects, fruit, and sugary foods, such as nectar from flowers and tree sap.

Echidna

The echidna, or spiny anteater *(right)*, is one of only a few mammals that lay eggs. After ten days, tiny babies hatch from the eggs. They feed on their mother's milk. The echidna's body has a protective covering of prickly spines, like a hedgehog. It eats insects, mainly ants and termites, which it licks up with its long, sticky tongue.

Bowerbird

This female bird *(above)* has been attracted to a display site, or bower, made by a male bowerbird from grass and twigs. To court a female, a male will decorate a bower with berries, feathers, and other bright objects. (Unfortunately, some bright objects, such as the blue bottle caps in this picture, can harm birds). Different species of bowerbirds build bowers of different shapes. Bowerbirds live in the forests of New Guinea and Australia.

Tree kangaroo

Like all kangaroos, a tree kangaroo *(right)* is a marsupial. A number of different species live in Australia and New Guinea. Some can hop on the ground like kangaroos of the outback. Others spend their entire lives in the trees and cannot hop. The long tail of the tree kangaroo helps it balance as it clambers among the branches. It is remarkably agile, despite not having feet adapted for climbing.

TEMPERATE RAIN FORESTS

Spotted owls
These owls *(above)* live in the cool, wet forests of North America. They rest in trees during the day and hunt at night for small rodents.

THE world's temperate rain forests are in cooler regions north and south of the tropics. The largest ones are on the northwestern coast of North America; on the southern tip of South America, in Chile; and on South Island in New Zealand. Temperate rain forests once covered twice as much land as they do today. Unfortunately, they thrived in places where the land was needed to grow crops or build roads and towns. In many regions, only small patches of temperate rain forests survive, on steep or rocky hillsides where the land is of little use for farming. The islands of Japan, for example, were once covered by cool rain forest. Now, only a tiny part of this forest survives, on the island of Yakushima. The trees that grow in temperate rain forests are prized by logging companies, and a great many have been cut down for timber. Temperate rain forests are home to a wide variety of animals, although fewer species than are found in tropical rain forests.

Kiwi
These strange, flightless birds are found only in New Zealand. Kiwi *(left)* live in burrows. They scurry around the forest floor at night sniffing out insects and worms to eat.

Kauri pines
This kauri pine *(left)*, named Tane Mahuta, or Lord of the Forest, is the largest in New Zealand. These trees can grow up to 180 feet (55 m) tall and live 2,000 years. They are found in cool forests on New Zealand's North Island.

Olympic National Park, Washington state

This cool rain forest has shrubs, ferns, mosses, and many types of trees. The northwestern coast of North America has high rainfall because it is swept by wet winds blowing in from the Pacific.

Mule deer

Mule deer *(right)*, are named for their long, mulelike ears. They roam the temperate forests of North America from Alaska to northern Mexico. These deer are shy creatures and are hard to spot among the forest trees.

Quolls

This tiger quoll *(below)* lives in the mountainous rain forests of Tasmania and eastern Australia. It is an aggressive marsupial with a spotted coat and survives by hunting birds, insects, and mammals.

Tasmanian devils

This ferocious animal can be found only on the island of Tasmania, which is off southern Australia. The western part of Tasmania is covered with temperate rain forest. The Tasmanian devil *(above)* lives in eucalyptus woods. It is the largest surviving, meat-eating marsupial. Up to 3 feet (1 m) long, it feeds mainly on dead animals, or carrion.

OBSERVING ANIMALS

THE animals of rain forests and other woodland areas are cautious and quick-witted. Their keen eyesight, sharp hearing, and good sense of smell allow them to sense you long before you know they are there. The only way to get close to forest animals is to be patient and stay very quiet and still.

In Madagascar, experts use radio transmitters to track lemurs and other animals.

MATERIALS

You will need: warm hat, scarf, gloves, binoculars.

When going out to observe animals, wear clothing that is dull-colored to blend in with the woods. Dress for the weather and always have an adult go with you. When you see an animal, move slowly and quietly. Stay behind the cover of trees or bushes. Do not get close to the animal. Sometimes the signs wild animals leave are easier to spot than the animals themselves. Animal homes, such as nests and burrows, are often easy to find, too. Hair, half-eaten food, and droppings all show that animals have been in the area.

Observing animals

1 When observing animals in the woods, move slowly and put your feet down carefully. Step softly on fallen leaves, which can rustle and give you away. Try to avoid dry twigs that might crack.

2 Stay behind the cover of trees or shrubs that will hide you from the animals. If you spot an animal, drop down on all fours and be very still.

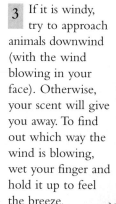

3 If it is windy, try to approach animals downwind (with the wind blowing in your face). Otherwise, your scent will give you away. To find out which way the wind is blowing, wet your finger and hold it up to feel the breeze.

Finding animal signs

1 A hole in a forest tree shows that a bird has nested there. This hole was drilled by a woodpecker. A field guide will have details about birds that nest this way.

2 Animals that burrow into the earth leave clear signs of their presence. These holes were made by rabbits. Fresh earth and droppings show that the burrow is in use.

3 Gnawed bark, half-eaten fruit, or broken twigs are all signs of animals feeding. The bark of this tree was gnawed by deer when food was scarce in winter.

M A T E R I A L S

You will need: gloves, notebook, pencil, magnifying glass, binoculars, field guide.

4 Some mammals sharpen their claws on tree trunks and leave scratch marks. These scratches were made by a badger. They show that this part of the forest is occupied.

5 Droppings, such as these left by a fox, show where animals have fed. Some animals leave droppings to mark their territory — the area where they hunt for food.

6 Look for animal fur caught in barbed wire or on the bottom of a wooden fence. Notice the color and texture of the hair. This hair belonged to a badger.

PEOPLE OF THE RAIN FOREST

THERE are about a thousand different tribes, or groups, of people living in rain forests around the world. Many of these tribes have lived in the forest for hundreds, or even thousands, of years. They take what they need from the forest without harming it. Some groups, such as the Yanomami of the Amazon basin and the Huli of New Guinea, gather fruit and vegetables and hunt animals for meat. Their tools and weapons are traditionally made from materials such as wood. Plants collected from the forest are used as medicines. Some groups grow gardens of crops around their villages. They farm in ways that do not destroy the forest. The well-being of many people who live in the rain forest is threatened by the ever-shrinking forest and by disease, logging, farming, and mining. In some rain forest countries, where governments have encouraged people from the cities to settle in the forest, the new settlers often farm in ways that harm the forest. They also bring diseases such as mumps and chicken pox, which can kill the local people.

Growing crops
Native people clear patches of forest to grow crops. Then they move on, allowing the forest to grow back.

Forest hunters
Amerindians are skillful hunters. They use traps, bows and arrows, and blowpipes that fire darts tipped with poison. Today, they also use guns, making these hunters even more efficient. This Amerindian (*left*) from the Amazon rain forest has killed an armadillo.

The Pygmies
Mbuti and Baka Pygmies live in the rain forests of Central Africa. Traditionally, they live by hunting and gathering food. This Pygmy woman (*left*) is cooking food outside her hut, with her baby asleep on her back.

Huli warriors
The Huli are one of many tribes in the remote highland rain forests of Papua New Guinea. They live by hunting, gathering plants, and growing crops. Men and women live apart, in large group houses. The men decorate their bodies with colored clay and wear elaborate headdresses for ceremonies.

Old and new
Like many groups living in the rain forests of Southeast Asia, the Lemenak still build houses made of traditional local materials, such as wood and bamboo. This grandmother *(above)* is weaving a basket from leaves, while looking after her grandaughter in a hammock made of more modern materials.

The Yanomami
One of the largest groups of Amerindian people in South America is the Yanomami. Their village life centers around the yano, or communal house. The yano is a large, circular building with a living space in the middle. It is constructed of vine and leaf thatch. This picture *(left)* shows Yanomami men eating a meal.

FACT BOX

• The Amerindians of South America once used the roots of jungle vines to make curare, a deadly poison for their arrows. Now scientists use curare to make a drug to relax muscles.

• The Brazilian rain forest has 140 different tribes, or groups, living there.

RAIN FOREST SHELTER

P EOPLE who live in the rain forests build their homes from materials found there, such as wood and leaves. Their houses provide protection from heavy rain and fierce jungle animals. In South America, the Yanomami's large, round huts are made from trees bent into a dome shape, lashed with vines, and thatched with palm leaves. The roofed area is used for sleeping. The Yanomami sleep in hammocks that hang from the rafters. The hammocks are made of woven grasses. You can build a simple shelter with a hammock by following the instructions below. This project requires careful thought and the help of an adult. When looking for branches, be sure an adult goes with you. Collect the branches from your yard or a nearby woods. Do not cut branches from trees; always gather them from the ground — where they have fallen naturally. Also, be sure that the branches are thick enough to support your weight.

Longhouses
In Peru, houses are built on stilts to guard against flooding. They are entered by a ladder that is pulled up at night. Large communal huts, called longhouses, might shelter as many as a hundred families.

Building a shelter

1 Securely tie the ends of two sturdy branches together with strong rope. Stand the branches upright to make an A-frame. Tie the A-frame to a tree for extra support.

2 Tie two more branches together and stand them upright about 6 feet (2 m) from the first A-frame. Place a lighter branch on top to make a ridgepole and tie it in place.

3 Attach two guylines to each of the A-frames. Stake the guylines securely in the ground. Then throw a tarpaulin over the ridgepole to form the roof.

4 Attach guylines to the eyeholes in the corners of the tarpaulin and stake them securely in the ground. Stretch the tarpaulin tight to make the roof.

5 Thread heavy string or cord through the eyeholes on opposite sides of the ground cloth to form a sort of tube. Push a pole into each side of the tube.

6 Pull the two poles apart to make a stretcher that will fit inside the shelter. This stretcher will be the hammock that you can rest on off the ground.

Make sure the hammock is secure and will not slip down the poles when your weight is on it. Now you can take a well-earned rest!

7 Wedge the stretcher inside the shelter with the poles resting on the outside of the upright A-frames.

RAIN FOREST PRODUCTS

Chewing gum
The sapodilla, or chicle, tree produces a milky sap that thickens when heated. The Aztecs chewed gum from the chicle tree. Our gum also comes from this rain forest tree.

THE world's tropical rain forests seem remote, but their products are all around us and are part of our everyday lives. Without rain forests, there would be no rubber, sugar, or chocolate. The next time you visit a supermarket, look at labels to see how many foods come from these forests. Bananas, lemons, pineapples, and avocados all come from tropical rain forests. So do many kinds of nuts, including peanuts, cashews, and Brazil nuts. Coffee beans and kola nuts are used to make coffee and cola drinks. Other rain forest plants produce spices, such as ginger, nutmeg, cinnamon, and pepper. All of these products come from plants that first grew wild in rain forests. Now many of them have been cultivated for the world market on large plantations. The rain forest also produces hardwoods, such as ebony, mahogany, and rosewood, that are used for building houses and making furniture. Unfortunately, when trees are cut down for timber or forests cleared for plantations, wild plants and animals suffer.

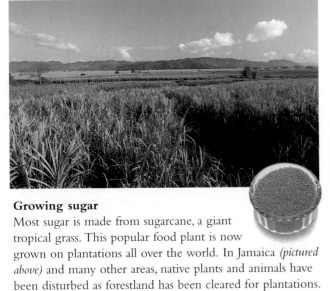

Growing sugar
Most sugar is made from sugarcane, a giant tropical grass. This popular food plant is now grown on plantations all over the world. In Jamaica *(pictured above)* and many other areas, native plants and animals have been disturbed as forestland has been cleared for plantations.

Oil palms
These young oil palms *(above)* in Costa Rica are being watered. Oil from the fruit of mature palms is used for cooking, as well as to make soap, shampoo, and cosmetics. Oil palms first grew in West Africa. Now they are found in tropical regions all over the world.

Bamboo

This worker *(right)* is harvesting bamboo by  cutting through the thick stems with a sharp knife called a machete. Bamboo is actually a kind of giant, fast-growing grass — not a tree. The tough stems of bamboo are used for building houses and as poles for scaffolding. Bamboo cane is used for weaving baskets, building furniture, and making musical instruments.

Rubber is dyed before it is molded into shape.

Rubber harvest

Natural rubber is made from a sticky sap, called latex, that oozes from the bark of rain forest trees. To harvest this sap, grooves are cut into the bark, and the latex runs down the grooves into a little cup hanging on the tree's trunk. Rubber is used to make a wide range of products, from hot water bottles and car tires to rubber bands and tennis balls.

Healing plants

Rain forests have long been a source of herbs and medicines for the people who live there. Scientists have discovered the medical benefits of only a small proportion of these plants and believe that many others will still be found. Quinine from the cinchona tree *(above)* is used to treat malaria and to make tonic water. The Madagascar periwinkle is used to treat a form of cancer called leukemia.

SAVING THE RAIN FORESTS

Tigers
Asian tigers *(above)* need a large area in which to hunt. As their forest habitat is destroyed, the number of tigers will drop.

THE world's rain forests are disappearing at a rate of 6,000 acres (2,428 hectares) every hour. When forests are cut down, the plants and animals that live in that habitat are put at risk. Scientists believe that much wildlife in the rain forests has not yet been discovered. They fear some species will die out before they have even been identified. What is being done to stop this destruction? People are starting to realize that rain forests are a vital resource for the whole world. We rely on them for many different products, including precious medicines. Rain forests affect the weather for hundreds of miles (km) around them, bringing rain and keeping the air well supplied with oxygen. Developed countries and rain forest nations now meet at international conferences to plan ways to conserve, or save, the rain forests. Many different things can be done. Forests can be managed more effectively, with controlled logging and the planting of new trees, and more national parks and reserves can be set up to protect wildlife.

Mountain gorillas
Gorillas *(right)* found in the upland rain forests of eastern Africa are a threatened species. They face a shrinking habitat and death by poachers. Reserves have been set up to try to save them.

Sumatran rhinoceros
This Sumatran rhino *(above)* is wallowing in a cool mud bath. Due to hunting and the destruction of its habitat, only a few hundred of these magnificent animals still survive in the wild. They can be found in the forests of Southeast Asia. Except for those left in zoos, these rhinos might soon die out altogether.

Planting trees

These seedlings at a nursery in Ghana *(right)* are trees that will be planted in the rain forest to replace those cut down for timber. Unfortunately, hardwood trees grow very slowly, and it will be many years before these young trees are forest giants. Another way to save rain forest trees is to use softwood timber to make furniture. Softwood trees grow much more quickly, so they are easier to replace.

Golden lion tamarins

These rare monkeys *(right)* are found only in coastal rain forests in South America. Forty years ago, they were close to extinction (dying out). People had killed the monkeys, mistakenly believing they spread disease. The survivors were bred in captivity in the United States and Europe. Now, golden lion tamarins have been released back into the wild.

Breeding orangutans

Orangutans (*at the left of the picture above*) are being fed in a breeding center in Borneo. Orangutans are large forest apes from Borneo and Sumatra. Their name means "man of the forest." Deforestation has threatened the survival of these apes, but they are now being bred in captivity. Tourists come to see these animals being raised and bring much-needed money to the area.

People power

This Amerindian *(left)* is protesting the destruction of the Amazon rain forest at an international conference. Many people who live in the rain forest have recently started demanding a say in what happens to the land. They fight plans to build new mines, roads, or dams in these areas if they feel the new development will harm their way of life.

GLOSSARY

algae – microscopic plants with no roots, stems, or leaves that cluster together by the millions and grow mostly in water and damp places.

browse – to casually eat grass and other plants, as in a pasture; to graze.

buttress roots – roots that grow up the sides of some very tall trees and flare out at the bottom to keep the tree upright.

camouflage – coloring, shape, or movement that hides something by making it blend in with its surroundings.

canopy – the topmost layer of leaves and branches that spreads over a rain forest.

carnivore – an animal that eats other animals; a meat eater.

carrion – the rotting flesh of dead animals.

chicle – a milky substance from the sapodilla tree that thickens when heated and is used to make chewing gum.

chlorophyll – the green coloring in plants that absorbs the sun's energy, which is needed for the process of photosynthesis to occur.

communal – owned and used by many people; shared by members of a group or community.

curare – a poisonous liquid that comes from jungle vines and is used by South American Indians for hunting and by scientists to make medicine that relaxes muscles.

deforestation – the cutting down, burning, and clearing of forestlands.

emergent – a tree that stands out above a forest's canopy.

epiphyte – a plant that lives on another plant and gets its water and nutrients from the air; an air plant.

erosion – the wearing away of soil or rock, usually by the action of wind or water.

estuary – a wide waterway at the lower end, or mouth, of a river, where ocean tides meet the river's current.

eyespot – a spot of color that looks like an eye.

festoon – (v) to drape or hang in loops or curves, as a garland, between two points that are above the ground.

glacier – an enormous mass of ice and snow that moves slowly down a mountain or across a vast area of land.

guyline – a rope or wire used to guide, brace, or hold something steady or securely to some kind of anchor.

habitat – a place or area with living and growing conditions that are, by nature, suitable for a particular animal or plant.

herbivore – an animal that eats only plants for food.

igapó – an area of swampy forestland in the lower Amazon basin that is permanently flooded.

mangrove – a tree found along tropical coastlines and river estuaries that grows special prop roots along its branches for support and to absorb oxygen from the air.

marsupial – belonging to an order of mammals in which the young are carried and nourished in a pouch on the abdomen of the female. A kangaroo is a marsupial.

montane – belonging to the moist and cool upper slopes.

naturalist – a person who studies nature, especially plants and animals.

omnivore – an animal that eats both plants and other animals.

parasitic – dependent on another organism to exist.

photosynthesis – the process by which green plants make their food, using energy from the sun to turn water and carbon dioxide into glucose (a simple sugar).

poacher – a person who kills or steals game illegally.

predator – an animal that hunts other animals for food.

preen – to clean, smooth, and tidy the feathers with a beak.

prehensile – able to grasp something by wrapping around it.

prey – (n) an animal hunted by other animals for food.

quadrat – a square- or rectangular-shaped plot of ground used by scientists who study the plants and animals found there.

root – (v) to search for or dig up with the snout.

stomata – microscopic holes on the underside of a plant's leaves through which carbon dioxide moves in and oxygen moves out during the process of photosynthesis.

thatched – covered with plant matter or other natural materials, such as grass, leaves, straw, or reeds.

transpiration – the process by which sunshine turns liquid water in the leaves of plants into water vapor that escapes into the air through stomata. The water vapor gathers in the air, and, when it is cooled, turns back into a liquid.

tropics – the region of Earth with a very hot, moist climate that extends about 23½ degrees both north and south of the equator, lying between the Tropic of Cancer in the north and the Tropic of Capricorn in the south.

understory – the layer of trees and plants growing between a forest's floor and its canopy.

várzea – forestland on the plains along the Amazon River that is flooded during the rainy season.

wary – watchful and cautious to avoid danger.

xylem – the tubelike tissue in the stems and trunks of plants and trees through which water is drawn upward into the plant.

BOOKS

Endangered! (series). Bob Burton (Gareth Stevens)

Environment Alert! (series). (Gareth Stevens)

In Peril (series). Barbara J. Behm and Jean–Christophe Balouet (Gareth Stevens)

Inside the Amazing Amazon: Incredible Fold-out Cross Sections of the World's Greatest Rainforest. Don Lessem (Crown Publishing Group)

Lost Forever (series). Barbara J. Behm and Jean–Christophe Balouet (Gareth Stevens)

Mangrove Wilderness: Nature's Nursery. Bianca Lavies (Dutton Children's Books)

The Mysterious Jungles. Andreu Llamas (Chelsea House)

Nature's Green Umbrella: Tropical Rain Forests. Gail Gibbons (William Morrow)

Rain Forests and Reefs: A Kid's-Eye View of the Tropics. Caitlin and Thane Maynard (Franklin Watts)

Rain Forests: Lush Tropical Paradise. Wonderworks of Nature (series). Jenny Wood (Gareth Stevens)

Temperate Forests. Biomes of the World (series). Elizabeth Kaplan (Marshall Cavendish)

Why Save the Rain Forest? Donald Silver (Simon & Schuster)

VIDEOS

Alaska's Rain Forest: The Tongass. (New Dimension Media, Inc.)

The Amazon: A Vanishing Rainforest. (The Cinema Guild)

America's Rainforest. (Cambridge Educational)

Buying a Rain Forest. (Beacon Films)

Can Tropical Rain Forests Be Saved? (PBS Home Video)

Ecology of a Temperate Ancient Rain Forest. (New Dimension Media, Inc.)

The Tropical Rain Forest. (Films for the Humanities & Sciences)

WEB SITES

natsafaris.com/index.htm

168.216.238.53/amazon/index.htm

Some web sites stay current longer than others. For further web sites, use your search engines to locate the following topics: *Africa, Amazon, Australia, ecology, epiphyte, marsupial, rain forest, toucan, tropics, Yanomami.*

INDEX

PICTURE CREDITS

b=bottom, t=top, c=center, l=left, r=right

Bruce Coleman Limited: 4r; 6tr, bl, br; 7t, bl; 8b; 9br; 10t; 12t, bl, br; 13t, br; 16br; 17bl, br; 18t; 21br; 24b; 25tr; 26br; 29t; 30tr; 32t; 33b, t; 36t; 37c, b; 38t; 39tr, br; 40t; 42bc, t; 43t, bl, br; 45bl, br; 47tl, bl, br; 48bl, br; 49tr, b; 50bl; 51t, br; 52bl, br; 53tr, cr; 55tr; 60bl; 62t. Ecoscene: 21tl. Garden & Wildlife Matters Photo Library: 29b. Holt Studios International: 28bl, 44br, 58t, 61c, 63tl. Hutchison Library: 56t, bl. Frank Lane Picture Agency: 9tr; 16t; 17t; 20t; 21bl; 25bl, br; 27tl; 28t, br; 29c; 34bl, bc, br; 44bl; 45tl; 46b; 48t; 50t, br; 53tl, b; 55tl, tc, bl, bc, br; 56br; 62bl; 63tr. Natural History Photographic Agency: 25tl; 36bl, br; 37t; 44t; 45tr; 54t. Natural Science Photos: 33c. Papilio Photographic Agency: 7br; 8t; 9tl; 13bl; 16bl; 39tl, bl; 42c; 46t; 49tl; 51bl; 57tr; 60br; 61tr, br; 62br; 63bl. Planet Earth Pictures: 24t; 32bl; 34t, 47tr. Still Pictures: 63br. Trip/J. Wakelin: 57tl. Zefa Pictures: 52t, 57b.